Honoring The Land

Honoring the Land

Anil Thapa

Standard Books

Honoring the Land
Copyright © 2019 by Anil Thapa

Additional copies may be ordered from the publisher for educational, business, promotional or premium use.

Book Design by Alex Johnson

ISBN 13
978-1-63132-082-8

Library of Congress Control Number: 2019919788

Library of Congress Cataloging-in-Publication Data
is available upon request.

First Edition

Published in the United States of America by Standard Books
an imprint of Advanced Publishing LLC

PRINTED IN THE UNITED STATES OF AMERICA

10 9 8 7 6 5 4 3 2 1

Welcome Note

The title, *Honoring The Land*, came to me when I was in the United States and heard about the Native American people who are also known as First Nation people. I deeply respect the Native American Indigenous communities and thank them from the bottom of my heart for keeping their wisdom, teachings, and traditions alive.

I am a Vajrayana practitioner, which means "esoteric Buddhist Practitioner." My practice includes carrying out rituals with elements, and the title, *Honoring The Land*, resonates because through honoring the land, we connect with Mother Earth and the elements of nature. I am also a Native American flute player and have an album with the same title, Honoring The Land. In the future, I hope to make a documentary that focuses on honoring the land through sacred art.

I do not know how my book will benefit the world, but I have a deep calling from my heart that is compelling me to write. I am so grateful that you will be joining me on this journey and I want to thank you for reading my story. I will take you through my life journey, and by witnessing me, I believe you will become part of my family. Through my story, I hope you will become one with your body, mind, and spirit.

Before we start, I would like you to pause, take three long deep breaths, and relax. Take a moment to be thankful for the elements of nature: Water, Fire, Air, Earth, and Space. Feel gratitude for the divine force from which all wisdom traditions come.

I have always enjoyed a cup of tea when reading and engaging in contemplative practices. I invite you to do the same as you continue reading.

About Me

My journey started with a childhood filled with poverty and challenge. I was the third child of four. I had two older brothers, Santosh and Krishna, and a younger sister named Sunita.

My father was a policeman, and my mother mainly cared for the family. My father often had to relocate for work, and we would have to follow him. My mother would tell us stories about the places we moved to when we were young, but I can only remember growing up in Bhaktapur. Known as the "City of Devotees," it is a magical place. The city is still dear to my heart, and if you ever get the chance to visit, I highly recommend it.

My father did not make much money as a policeman, and we struggled financially. We could not afford to own a home and were forced to rent wherever we moved. Sometimes it was hard for my parents to pay the rent, and I have memories of landlords giving us a hard time. Coming from a low-income family, my parents could not afford to send us to school. None of my siblings received an education.

We lived near a place where tourists would frequent, and my elder brother learned he could make money by interacting with the tourists and showing them around town. The money he earned brought him some stability, but he spent most of his time and money drinking. In this, he followed in our father's footsteps. Alcoholism ran in our family, and my father struggled with it the most. It put a lot of strain on the family, and my mother suffered because of it.

Since then, a lot has changed for the better. My father managed to stop drinking, my parents now own a house that I built for them, and both my brothers are happily married. Even though things are far more stable for my family, the memories of hardship are still with us.

Growing up in difficult circumstances, I always knew things

would change, but I did not know how or when. I have come to realize that when you are in a dark stage of life, it's hard to see the light.

My goal is to help others see life differently, in simple ways, and re-connect to Mother Nature as a way of moving through the darkness, back into the light.

Because my father was a policeman, he wanted me to also serve in the police force or army, but I knew that path was not mine. I had a different calling. Growing up in the sacred town of Bhaktapur, I always felt some universal energy that gently pulled me in a different direction. It whispered in my ear, and it took quite some time before I learned how to listen, but when I did, I realized it wanted me to become a Dharma Warrior.

When I was young, I learned about Thangkas, a sacred Buddhist artform, but I did not understand its meaning or the teachings behind it.

I went to school for a short time but found it so uninspiring, all I wanted to do was play in nature and connect with the elements. Following my heart, I left school and focused on studying the art and culture of my country.

As we all know, life is a journey that can take us in the most unexpected directions. At this stage in my life, I am drawn to explore internal states; as the Buddha said, "The universe inside oneself is waiting to be revealed."

I hope to reignite our connection to Mother Nature, as that pathway of rediscovery is one of creativity and joy. Along that path, we can protect our environment and save Mother Nature for future generations. When we cultivate care for nature, it naturally increases the compassion in our hearts, and when we commit to protecting our environment, it is not just for our benefit, but for all animals and sentient beings.

I feel honored to share my journey along this path and hope it will inspire others to take similar steps and contribute to this cause.

Introduction

We are all energy and frequency, and what we cultivate inside is what we emanate and express externally.

It is essential to be aware of what is going on in both our internal and external environments. No matter our circumstances, cultivating gratitude and awareness of breath connects us more to our hearts and helps us live harmoniously within our environment. The power of life is connected to our breath, and breath is life. That is why it's called "Prana."

There is a story about a group of people who, when asked, "Who wants change?", everyone raised their hands. But when asked, "Who wants to be the change?" few raise their hands.

It's funny how we all desire change, but when it becomes personal, it can be challenging to act upon that desire. When we take responsibility for our emotions, habits, and states of being, we begin to become the change we seek.

One of the fascinating teachings of Buddhism is not to think about changing the world, but to be aware of our own actions and thoughts, which then creates the momentum for change.

One path to self-awareness and change in our lives is possible through the practice of honoring the land and connecting to nature.

One of the most important aspects of life is breath. Without it, we would not exist. Breathing can be a portal to deep parts of Self; it strengthens our conscious alignment with Prana.

How often do you sit in silence, while out in nature, allowing your surroundings wash over you? How often do you let yourself rest on the land and listen to the birds and feel the wind?

When you seek refuge amongst the trees and connect to what the forest has to offer, you can tap into the universal harmony of nature. This aspect of elemental balance is often missing in modern life.

The origins of true harmony come from an internal state of being, and the practice of connecting to the elements of nature allows this internal state to bloom.

There are several aspects of both Buddhism and shamanism that intersect. Buddhism signifies a journey of self-understanding, whereas shamanism represents connecting to spiritual experiences through accessing the natural world and energetic realms.

If major religions openly embraced nature and emphasized protecting it, we would become more connected to the natural world. This would help awaken humanity.

And while we all value our cultural traditions, if we embraced honoring the land and respecting the elements as a society, we would create a conscious shift towards harmony.

Indigenous peoples around the world are and have always been intimately connected to nature and the wisdom of working with the elements. We can learn from their ancient knowledge, and by following their path of honoring the land, we can rediscover harmony.

Honoring the Land

Some stories claim that human beings came to Earth, some say billions of years ago, from other planets, but this hasn't been proven. One thing we do know is, we experience joy and peace by living in harmony with the elements.

Everyone on Earth is mortal—even the Buddha and other enlightened beings left this world to show that what comes must also go. That is the circle of life.

Let us focus on five things:

1) Take a few deep breaths and observe our breathing and be thankful for it.

2) Let us contemplate and pay tribute to our parents, who gave us birth.

3) Gratitude to the five elements: air, earth, fire, water, space.

4) Gratitude for all the enlightened teachers who have led us to light.

5) The Bodhisattva who work for the benefit of all beings.

You might be curious about the meaning of Bodhisattva. They are beings who give up their happiness to help end the suffering of others. I will share more about Bodhisattva later.

This book is about honoring the elements and being grateful.

As you turn each page, remember to look around and be aware of the world around you, and have gratitude in your heart.

In the last few years, I have spent a lot of time in the forest and in nature. These are the places where I receive inspiration to write, and I am thankful to share my thoughts about that experience with you.

As life goes on, we occasionally come to points where our awareness is more active because of troubles going on in our minds and outside. That said, if one can see that difficulties are but a part of life and one's journey through it, then those challenges become wisdom.

We may think that wisdom comes from outside, but it comes from within. And most of the time, it is formed when we experience failure or tragedy.

I have spoken with people who had accidents or experienced some tragic loss, who told me the event opened their consciousness into a different understanding of reality.

When a tragedy occurs, one can descend into a dark place, even to the point of considering suicide. In my own life, until the age of about fourteen, life was so dark that I only survived because I reminded myself that it would change and that I needed to be patient. The most difficult part was I did have any support so I was sad and afraid.

Because I know what it is like to be in a dark stage of life I want to support others who may be experiencing similar challenges while on their journey of transformation.

The solution for most of the problems in the world that is we need to reconnect to the elements of the Earth; to the mountains, rivers, wind, and land.

I am on a my transition leaving the united stated moving back to Nepal and also preparing for my retreat as a part of life journey and hopefully create a space for everyone to come and connect the land and the elements .

As I have run and still while I am writing this book the lumbini Buddhist Art Gallery in Berkeley California.

I am meeting so many amazing people who share their life journey with me for example I just met this guy on a wheel chair and he was tell me his story as he was diving in the ocean he somehow got drawn and kind a died and he was telling me he sow like a bigger picture of himself beyond the physical body, interesting things is he was telling me that its not about any kind of light he sow but its like he become one with the all the

elements for that reason I want share this here in my book because this is my practice its to become one with the elements.

Most of yogis of past and real yogis if you see they really direct you towards nature for understanding for your own nature
of mind. Like yesterday when I was sitting In the forest near the
waterfall there a leaf falling and looking at that makes me very
happy and this is what we are looking for a true answer of life
is found in the nature phenomena to teach you there is beauty
and there is chaos , and those both are the part of nature existence.

These yogis in the past and of course there are many yogis
in many traditions I would like to share about the yogi who was
criminal after became a great yogi who attain enlightenment in
one life time his name was Milarepa and as his realization and
says

Deep in the wild mountains, is a strange marketplace, where
you can trade the hassle and noise of everyday life, for eternal
Light.

If one wants to grow and help others, it is essential to honor
the land and connect with the elements first.

Many want to change the world, but to do so, we must
change ourselves by taking care of daily life and adding compassion to life's path.

If your journey lacks compassion, it is a journey of frustra-
tion. Change yourself first and see what happens.

Everyone wants to protect the fish in the ocean, but no one
wants to stop eating fish.

When I was a child, small things guided me, like playing outside with other children. Being out in nature, we had lots of fun.
And it is still magical when we go out, into the forest and listen
to the wind and birds.

Every time I go camping, there are families with the kids; I
always notice how they seem to become more alive when they
are outside, connected with land and trees.

I once knew a child who instead of going to school, spent most of his time in the forest where he learned to speak the language of birds. He shared how magical it is when we are connected with nature.

I encourage you to spend more time outdoors, in nature, so that you can discover the magic in life. I have no doubt magic happens everywhere, but in nature, where the trees and rivers are, people connect with the land, and with that connection, profound things happen.

I want to acknowledge and thank the First Nation peoples of America who know how to live in harmony with Mother Nature, as well as the white Americans who came later who founded modern America.

These First Nation peoples of American are known as "wisdom keepers." They have the wisdom to live in harmony with Mother Nature—something we are losing in the modern world.

When I came to United States, one of the first things I did was search for a First Nation tribe. It was amazing how some of their people seemed so similar to the shamans of my homeland, Nepal.

The solutions to many problems we have in the world can be found through honoring the land.

We will have all the answers we need through a connection with the land.

Even Buddha became enlightened while sitting under a tree. His final battle was with what is called the "Mara," or "disturbing emotion." He conquered this disturbing emotion by touching Mother Earth. This became known as *bhumisparsa mudra*.

In some parts of the world, where there are high buildings and advanced technology, many people lack a connection with the land and elements.

The biggest problem in the world is not a physical problem; it's a mental problem. It is so severe, for some, it leads to suicide. In some modern countries, like Japan, for example, suicide is a real problem. Any country that does not value nature has not only environmental problems, but serious mental health problems too.

Even as I write this book, I am learning to connect with the land, as I walk barefoot so I can feel the land.

There are many reasons why we should connect with the land. One is to honor our ancestors and be grateful for them.

People leave trash on the beach and throw it in rivers, where animals only leave footprints. I suppose human beings are evolving, and they will learn in time how to care for the land.

What happened? Why and when we forget that we must co-exist with nature? If we don't successfully co-exist, we only create hell for ourselves and others. The way to create heaven on Earth is to connect back to land and honor it.

Developing gratitude is the fundamental medicine for our many sufferings.

Modern science proves that positive thinking changes our hormones, which then creates positive energy that is good for us and others.

Depending solely upon technology can be the very cause of our problems, although we can use technology to share our positivity with others. Everything is part of creation and everyone is on a journey of understanding. We may all be on different paths, but we will eventually be at the same point.

Sometimes, as life goes on, we become too busy trying to keep up with the modern world—a world that demands many things. We age without fully understanding the meaning of life or fulfilling our true propose in life.

For many people, wisdom arises only in old age, after much life experience.

Meditation is becoming more popular in the West because it slows people down, and helps them understand themselves.

There is a meditation practice called *vipassana*. It involves observing one's breathing and not being judgmental. It allows thoughts to arise naturally and dissolve into space.

Most of the problems we have in life involves being too judgmental and forgetting to connect to the land.

Spending time in nature every day is different from going there once in a while. Sometimes we think we don't have time, but we must learn to play at times. If we make the effort to do so, time will guide us in play. One should find time to play, just as he does

for eating and sleeping. It should be part of our existence and life.

Self-awakening Journey

My awakening journey started when I started playing out in the woods. Something I heard from the wind and saw merging with the elements is what makes me ultimately happy.

Looking at a tiny drop of water on a leaf is so beautiful and magical. I love playing in the fog and listening to the wind. There is a saying that "Magic happens in the forest." It's true!

I grew up in a beautiful town with many temples and gods, and am blessed to have them as my friends. It was difficult for me to fit into society because of my background. My parents came from a village where my father was a policeman, and my mother spent most of her time taking care us. When I was a child I did not want to go to school. I knew there was a different kind of education for me; one I found through Buddhist Art Thanka.

Thangka Art taught me to take responsibility for my emotions and to be aware of them—something I am still working on.

My fears, insecurities, and confusion decreased when I started thangka painting and learning Buddhist philosophy.

I offer my deepest thanks to Jog Bhadur Gauchan Brother, who helped me on my journey. He is like my "karma parent"

who guided me on my path and helped me to believe in myself
and my path. I will always be thankful for his guidance and support.

Life is like an ocean. One must learn to swim and when we
find an island we can rest. Some people we meet in life are like
islands. We can trust them and rest.

My awakening happens in nature, and Thangka Art supports
me. And Gauchan Brother helped me establish a foundation to
stand upon.

Self-awakening is to be open to possibilities; to know oneself
better and grow. It is not necessary to explain everything to
everyone as we all see things differently.

Self-awakening happens to people in different ways. Sometimes it happens because of a tragedy or accident and sometimes
during meditation. Whenever it happens it's impotent to see
things differently, so that we can help others.

Self-awakening is a magical process because you see things
differently, as everyone is on their own journey.

You don't need to explain to anyone when you are on a journey of awakening, as your message will be known when your
awakened life is integrated into your daily activities.

The reason we become frustrated at times is we have the ex-
pectation people should understand us, but sometimes they
don't. But that's okay because the journey of life is not to explain
but live, And that is the path of true awakening; if you are frustrated, remember it is because you are trying to explain your life
to others and you are not yet fully understand the awakening
part of the journey.

When I was a child I liked spending time with elderly people,
asking them what is life like for them? Most would reply that
life is interesting. They would speak about exploration, devotion, and so on,

I have always been curious about what people think about
life, and now I see that life is many things for many people.

Everyone thinks about it at in many different ways.

One thing Buddhism answers about life is that no one wants to suffer and everybody wants happiness. We are all trying to be happy but we choose different paths to find it.

Because we all want happiness and do not want to suffer, how we apply ourselves in life to be happy is the very essence of our whether we attain it or not. We cannot expect apples when we plant bananas.

In my case, self-awakening happened when I was experiencing insecurity in my life; finances, family, food, and so on. Through that, I learned that wisdom only comes via the rough road; only through experience. Knowledge can be acquired from external sources, but wisdom comes only through understanding and experience.

My Childhood

My childhood was unstable. According to Buddhism it is my karma.

Unstable means I was a sick child. My parents fought all the time. My father was an alcoholic so when I think of my childhood, I remember that I saw no light—no possibilities of any way out from our circumstances. It was an intense period for me, and my brothers and sister. I did not have healthy childhood.

One of the teachings of Buddhism that I experience in my life is that everything changes; nothing stays the same. I now have a house, my parents are not fighting, my brother is doing well, and my sister is married. All of these changes occurred despite my having had a difficult childhood.

No matter what the circumstances, please remember everything will change. Be patient.

Most of my childhood I spent playing outside with mud and

plants, and I have memories about those times that I want to share. Let us reconnect to Mother Nature in whatever way possible, and let us honor the times we succeed at reconnecting.

This book is about more than my life, and I want to encourage everyone to go outside and listen to the wind; to spend more time in nature.

My childhood was a wild ride, and thinking about that makes me feel a little sad. But I am also grateful, mostly to my mother. As I mentioned before, I was a very sick child, so there were times when my mother took care of me and made sure I didn't die. I almost feel as though my mother gave me a new life—a second life. When most people thought I would die, my mother did not give up and took care of me. She gave me another life. so I dedicate my life to my birth mother and Mother Earth.

Everyone in this world has a story, but it's all about how we share it with the world. I share through my flute music, my art, and my book, and I hope to someday do so by way of a documentary film about connecting with the land.

Hopefully, after my retreat, I will be able to travel around the world and help people connect with Mother Nature.

Childhood is a time of learning, and I am looking forward to sharing my teachings with school children and college students. I look forward to helping them connect with themselves and nature.

Childhood memories and traumas can be strong, and, at times, it is difficult to manage. But through nature, we can bring balance to most everything.

Exploration

Curiosity and exploration are part of life. After traveling to several countries, I realize we all are looking for one thing: to be happy.

Something I find to be out of balance with human evolution is that we take nature for granted. Humankind demolishes what is natural to erect buildings. Evolution will improve when we become grateful and learn to live in harmony with nature.

One of the most significant issues we face in many developed countries today is depression.

Thinking that materialism can satisfy all needs is an illusion—one we have created, been told, or taught.

When I was young I learned about Christopher Columbus. I was taught that he was an explorer. But when I came to the United States, I also learned that he is now also seen as a kind of a invader who largely ended up being partially responsible for the destruction of much of Native American culture, similar to how the British East India Company came as friends to India then ruled for almost 200 years.

These explorations were not what we would today consider "real" exploration. Real exploration is when we honor other cultures and develop our experience by learning about them.

We should be curious, but we must understand that we are not superior in this world. We need to be kind and respect other beings and creatures who share the Earth with us.

My spiritual exploration began in Nepal in my town where we have 33 million gods. In Hinduism there are many many gods and goddesses and it's amazing that each one has its place.

The majority of Hindu people in Nepal believe in Buddhism because he was from a Hindu family and found a profound path to self-awakening that could share with others.

In the town where I grew up, there were also Christians and Muslims, and we all lived in harmony together.

In Nepal, the oldest tradition and practice is shamanism. It is perhaps the oldest practice throughout the world, as praying and working with the elements began long before all other religious traditions and philosophies.

Even in modern countries, people realize it seems this does not work, and we cannot live like this now, nor in the future.

As people become more aware, they desire and seek sustainable, harmonious ways of living with Mother Nature. Often, when the economy is booming, it is at the expense of our environment and nature. This is unhealthy. We must ask ourselves, "Is this really working?" We need to find a healthy way to live.

If humans are kind, we have God inside. If we are not kind, we develop the devil inside. It is important to check within and ask frequently, "Do I have God inside or the devil?"

The true exploration is when we understand our self and know what is inside.

We may be this or that and follow this tradition or that tradition, but ultimately it is important to understand the true self, for you, and for the sake of others.

May we travel and have more passion for exploration and curiosity, with compassion in our hearts, not greed.

Connection

When we enter the spiritual world, the whole point is to find a connection to the world around us.

According to Buddhism, the three primordial emotions of greed, ignorance, and anger, block our true nature. These three emotions are unhealthy.

The fundamental practice of Buddhism is to change these emotions into love, generosity, and wisdom.

This means everything is related. What is happening in my life is my karma, and what is happening in your life is your karma. Karma translated is "dependent origination."

If we want to know our connection to the world we have to take every action as mindfully as possible. This is not easy, however, as even Buddha Shakyamuni needed many lifetimes to reach enlightenment.

Connection to everything begins with a simple act. The 8th Century Tantric Master, Guru Padmasambhava, said:

If you want to know your past life, look at your present condition. If you want to know your future life, look at your present actions.

People often say, "We are connected to this and that," but if we do not take the first step of taking responsibility, we have misunderstood the meaning of connection.

There are many ways to become connected. Some are spiritual. Some connections happen because of accidents in life that break all the barriers of illusion—the ones that stand in our way, preventing us from meeting people or visiting places.

We have to keep questioning ourselves: What real connection do we seek?

The real connection we are looking for is within. We always have it. It is our shadow, with us all the time.

We just need to take a moment to say, "Hi," or find a way to connect within ourselves.

Real connections are when we cut mental barriers and reject limitations. We stop saying things like, "I am 'only' this or that…" While sometimes it may be appropriate to be "grounded" like a tree, but eventually we need to find a way to see our ultimate connection with everything. In this way, we can see the vast horizon of our consciousness.

Science confirms that everything is connected, so now, only our minds need to be open to see and feel that connection of oneness with everything.

The best gift you can offer the world is to understand yourself. In your journey of self-connection, I send you my best wishes.

BODDHICHITTA

Out of few words in Sanskrit, some are the most important words in my life. One I want to share with you is "bodhichitta." The supreme good heart is bodhichitta. "Bodhi" is the Sanskrit word for "enlightenment," and "chitta" is the word for "mind;" therefore, "bodhichitta," literally, means "mind of enlightenment."

Of all Dharma realizations, bodhichitta is supreme. This profoundly compassionate concept is the very essence of the Bodhisattva's training. Developing bodhichitta enables us to perfect all our virtues, solve all our problems, fulfill all our wishes, and develop the power to help others in the most appropriate and beneficial ways.

It is said that all the enlightened masters achieve enlightenment through bodhichitta and it is the base for spiritual practice.

Without a good foundation, one cannot grow, so it is critical to find the ground in our hearts so we can find the ground when we walk in nature.

When a tree is deeply grounded, it is free to grow and expand. That's what we are looking for. We need both grounding and expansion.

By having compassion in our hearts, we build a solid foundation. We ground ourselves and find ways to help others.

According to Mahayana (one path of Buddhism), all sentient beings have been our parents in our past lives, so Bodhichitta is the aspiration for self-awakening.

Bodhichitta prayer:

O precious and sublime bodhicitta,
May it arise in those in whom it has not arisen,
May it never decline where it has arisen,
But go on increasing, further and further!

Bodhisattva

The bodhisattva—the renowned ideal of Mahayana Buddhism—is
not a god or deity but a way of being we can all aspire to.

A bodhisattva is a person who lives in the spirit of Buddhism's bod-
hisattva vow, committing to put others before oneself, to give up one's own
well-being — even one's own enlightenment — for the sake of others.

The bodhisattva vow is the commitment to put others before
oneself.

It is a statement of willingness to give up one's well-being,
even one's enlightenment, for the sake of others. A bodhisattva
is a person who lives in the spirit of that vow, perfecting the
qualities known as the six *paramitas* [perfections] —generosity,
discipline, patience, exertion, meditation, and transcendental
knowledge—in his effort to liberate all beings.

There are many Bodhisatva in many traditions and cultures,
including Buddhism bodhisattvas, Avalokiteshvara, Vajrapani,
Manjushri, White Tara, and Green Tara.

Working with others is inspiring. We no longer try to build
up our grandiosity but rather become human beings who are
genuinely able to help others; that is, we develop selflessness—
something generally lacking in our world. Following the example of Gautama Buddha, who gave up his kingdom to work with
others, we finally become useful to society.

Taking a bodhisattva vow means we are inspired to put the
teachings of Buddhism into practice. In doing so we are mature
enough not to hold anything back. Our talents are utilized as
part of the learning process and practice.

A bodhisattva may teach dharma in the form of intellectual understanding, artistic understanding, or even business understanding. By committing ourselves to the bodhisattva path, we employ our talents in an enlightened way; we are not threatened or confused by them. Previously, our talents may have been "trips"—part of the texture of confusion—but now they are productive in a positive way. With patience, they can soon blossom with the help of a teacher. However, this does not mean there won't be challenges. Confusion will still occur. But there is also unlimited potential for growth and positive change.

Thanka Art

My interest in Thangka Art began about almost 18 years ago. When I was young, I wanted to be a physiologist. I am very interested in understanding the mind and life in general, and someone told me, "If you want to be physiologist, study your own mind."

When I heard that, I wondered if it was possible.

I grew up in a town in Nepal, where the Tamang people paint Thangka paintings. I was born in a warrior clan, so I thought being an artist was not in my blood.

Even though I was not born in an artistic, Buddhist family, I began selling Thangka Art at a gallery in Bhaktapur, Nepal. During my sales career, I only knew the story of Thangka Art, but not how to create it. Learning that took some time.

Thangka paintings help me see things differently; with a Buddhist view that recognizes our full potential as enlightened beings.

After seeing life from a different perspective, I began painting.

In the world of Thangka paintings, I am still a beginner. I am as a child, learning every day the symbols, attributes, expressions, colors, and significance of the work.

In my painting, I integrate the teachings of Buddhism, espe-cially tantric teaching of Buddhism called Vajrayana. I also do this in my daily life, realizing that walking the path is different than knowing the path.

As is always the case in learning and integrating, there are many ups and downs in painting, just as there are in life.

The propose of Thangka Art is to recognize the nature of the mind.

Thangka Art is like a reflection of our emotions and mind. It reveals, for example, the appearance of wrathful deities. A unique aspect of Vajrayana Buddhism is how it transforms dark-ness and negativity into luminous wisdom. Within Vajrayana meditation practice, wrathful deities are welcome as intense and overwhelming destroyers of ego.

Opening to the wrathful deities becomes a way to face our deepest fears and become free of them.

About Thangka Paintings

Thangka or THAN-KA is a Tibetan word for "Painted-Scroll," descended from the Pauba Art from Nepal.

They are painted on cotton canvas, using iconography based on ancient texts.

Thangkas are Buddhist art that abides by strict rules written in an ancient text, passed down from generation to generation. Significant

study is required to paint a Thangka; each ornament, pos-ture, and attribute represents a particular aspect of Buddhism and its teachings.

Introduction to Buddhist Art

Painting a Thangka requires considerable skill. The first step in any Thangka is to prepare the canvas. After that, the artist sketches the motif that he has decided to paint, then applies the color, shading, and finally, the gold.

The final and most crucial step is painting the facial features. This is often left to the "Guru" or "Master," as it is the most sacred part of the Thangka.

Each painting tells a unique story.

The iconography of the Thangka is rich in information about the spiritual practice of Buddhists.

A Thangka can help mediators learn about and emulate the qualities of a particular deity or visualize a path towards enlightenment. It can bring blessings on the household and serves as a constant reminder of the Buddha's teachings of compassion, kindness, and wisdom. Thangkas of particular deities are sometimes used for protection or to overcome obstacles.

Thangka's Connection with Mother Nature

There is a documentary entitled "Thongdrol," which means "liberation through seeing." Produced under the guidance of the 17th Karamapa, it is impressive and touching. It explains the value of connecting to nature and the elements of water, air, earth, fire, and space. These ancient forms of Thangka Art remind us to take care of our environment and the elements.

Thangka Art has been my road map in life, helping me connect back to nature. Seeing this documentary s a blessing.

When we are walking on the spiritual path, we see not only

walking, but also collective consciousness. That is how we connect with people.

Every artist makes Thangka Art differently. When I sit down, I give my mind, body, and spirit permission to align.

When I paint hills, clouds, or rivers, I become one with the painting.

We are all made of elements and there are many ways to connect to the elements. In my case, it was Thangka Art. I will try my best to explain as much as possible about Thangka Art that I hope you will find helpful and will find a way to reconnect with the elements yourself.

Thangka Art is a visual image of the enlightened nature of the mind, surrounded by the elements. Our mind and nature is then reflected in the form of Thangka art.

The first level of understanding Thangka Art is just regular art for art's sake. At the second level, we realize it's the reflection of different emotions. The third level is where we recognize it's the ultimate nature of the mind.

It is an honor for me to be able to explain and share some information about this sacred art.

Thangka Exhibitions Around the World

When I started Thangka Art I did not think I would be traveling abroad. I met Cindy, my partner and wife, in Nepal in 2012.

She was from the United States but was living in China at the time with her three children. Cindy was interested in doing an exhibition around end of 2012, so we did our first Thangka Art exhibition in Shanghai, China. It was well-received, so after that successful exhibition, we did few private shows at the Imperial Art Museum in Beijing.

My second exhibition was in June 2014 in Vancouver, Canada, with a dear friend, Joey Chan, whom I had met in my gallery in Nepal.

She was happy to share my art with her community in Canada, where it was also well received. At that show, many people saw Thangka art for the first time, so I felt thankful and blessed for the opportunity to share my art beyond my country.

After Canada, I went to see Cindy, as she had moved from Shanghai to Berkeley, California. We did another Nepalese Thangka Art exhibition in November 2014 that was well-received but not commercially successful.

Cindy and I loved working together. We married in 2015 and started our own gallery in Berkeley, California.

Since 2013 I have traveled back and forth to Nepal almost every six months to bring my work from the Lumbini Buddhist Art Gallery in Bhaktapur, Nepal, to Berkeley, California.

I recently decided to move back to Nepal to continue my spiritual meditation journey at a monastery in Nepal.

Life is an exciting journey, and I expect to learn many things on this journey.

Having first Thangka Art gallery in Berkeley California has been a blessing. I have met so many beautiful people; many times it feels as though I have known them for a long time.

Life in Berkeley

Berkeley is beautiful.

In my six-year journey so far, our Thanka gallery here has hosted nearly 200 events for the community and it is now like a community center.

Life in Berkeley is excellent, but I have come to the realization this is not the place I want to make my home, so I have decided to move back to Nepal.

There are many great things about Berkeley. One of them is I live close to nature where I love to spend as much time as possible, by myself or with friends.

Another blessing I received came by discovering the Native American flute in 2015. Since then, it has been part of my life, and I play almost every day.

I have come to realize that one of the healing methods I offer to the world is the sound and of my flute.

In the past six years, Cindy and I have visited many places, on camping trips and such.

When I moved here, I wanted to learn the "American Way." Cindy has three children from her previous marriage, so it took us some time to learn to work together.

Sadly, after many ups and downs and trying to make things work, we decided to separate.

Right now,
I am not happy or sad; I am just observing.
Buddha said, "You become what you think."

The world is like a Mandala and we are all living inside that Mandala. Externally, there are some places with more energy than others. Mt. Shasta, here in California, is one such place. I have been there almost ten times, and every time I go there I feel like I am back home.

According to Native Americans, Mt. Shasta is a sacred mountain, and I feel that when I am there. I feel a sense of welcoming, grounding and reconnecting when I am there.

Mt Shasta is like my mother who gives me love that I can then share with others.

I also found a cave in Tilden Park where I practice meditation. It too has been a blessing—to sit in that cave and connect back to nature.

Meeting beautiful, crazy people in Berkeley and being so

close to nature is such a blessing. I was once walking in the hills when I saw three deer with horns. Such a blessing! I encounter many things while on my path of enlightenment; some bless me by teaching me to be patient.

One of the greatest lessons I learned while in Berkeley is that for some in America, as is true everywhere, life can be either Heaven or Hell, depending upon what one values. You can suffer physically or mentally by seeking "things" that are not in alignment with your values. As the Dali Lama says,

"If you have a million dollars, without inner peace, you will be poor in spirit." Greed can turn a king into a beggar, and generosity can make a beggar a king. It's all about one's state of mind.

Sometimes, people try to write a book about one's entire life story, like that of Shakyamuni Buddha. How is that possible?

This book is not the answer you are looking for. The solutions to your problems are inside yourself, and I hope this book will help you find a path for your inner journey.

I was recently honored by city of Berkeley for creating a community space that share my art and culture with the Bay Brea.

Being honored by the city of Berkeley was a great way of celebrating with my friends and everyone who supported the gallery.

This will be my last year in Berkeley, and I am grateful for every experience there. It has been a time of growth and learning for me.

A few weeks ago I went swimming in the middle of the forest, in Lake Anza. I spent almost five hours there. It's an amazing place in nature, and every time I go there, I feel connected. It is a divine, magical union, of nature and spirit.

Water Elements

After describing Thangka Art and my journey, I will now focus on the elements and how we can align with them.

The world is made of different elements, the major ones being Fire, Water, Wind, Earth, and Space. In some traditions, there is wood and metal too, but these are part of Earth.

Each element has an aspect and value in creating the beauty of life.

When I am sitting next to a small creek, I see the water flowing so gentle and calm. It flows into the river and then eventually to the ocean. It then evaporates and forms fog, then clouds. It falls back to Earth as rain, again creating the creeks and rivers, and so on, over and over again.

When I was a child, I learned about the river, Nile, in Egypt. More than just a river of water, it has its own history and story. Rivers are like the veins in our bodies; if they are blocked, the body—the Earth—will have problems. We need to let the river flow to be in harmony.

Water is the source of life, and over 80% of the human body is water.

If we don't care for water how can we imagine living in a healthy way?

Nowadays there are big companies that want to make rivers and water private.

Like missionaries, they go to different countries and teach people a better way to live, but often destroy the art and culture of the region. This is what happened to the Native American people.

Every element is important so when we talk about them, we must not only look outside but within ourselves.

Every one of us is the manifestation of all these elements, and through self-awareness we create balance within ourselves and others.

There are many names for water in many languages. One fundamental similarity is that when everyone is thirsty, they only think of water.

I want share with you an event that happened during my stay in the United States.

A gas company was trying to build a pipeline on the sacred land of Native Americans in North Dakota. There was a fight, and American military forces came to disrupt the Native American activists who were protesting and protecting the land.

A Prayer for the Precious Gift of Water

Without water, we would die. Water is essential for life on Earth, not just human life but all life. Water is needed for drinking, cleaning, washing, and making crops grow. There is no substitute for this precious resource, and yet we waste it, we pollute it, and we even commodify it! Let's start anew, and begin by thanking the universe for the gift of water.

"Mother Ganga." This is the name given in Vedic. "Water" in Vedic Sanskrit and classical Sanskrit is "*ap*," also called "*ApaH*."

In Sanskrit there are at least a few hundred words for "water."

With many names and qualities to fulfill the desires of human life with its life force,

To the divine energy of water, I bow again and again.

Thank you for your gift that fills the gap in our body and Earth with the flow of blessings.

May we not block you but let you flow and share your blessings with the whole world.

Polluting is polluting our own bodies .
Thank you, Divine Mother, for your unconditional love.

Wind Elements

"Wind" is an interesting element for me because my name, Anil, means "god of the wind" in Sanskrit Vedic.

For nearly 25 years, I did not know the meaning of my name. I thought it was just a name, and to everyone who asked me about it, I would say its just a name.

Then, few years ago, I searched the meaning of Anil and I found that it is derived from Sanskrit ०००० (anila), meaning "air" or "wind." It is also another name, "Vayu," the Hindu god of the wind.

The wind element is the life force called "Prana" in Sanskrit and "Chi" in Chinese. This force is essential to our existence, for without prana or wind, we would not be breathing and life would not exist.

Physical Air is mostly represented as Wind, or Air in motion. Wind cannot be seen, although it can be felt.

Wind cannot be held, captured, or tamed. The invisible mover of things we can clearly see, the Wind influences the weather, the seasons, and therefore in a sense the essence of time itself.

Wind can be destructive as easily as it can be soothing. Wind can as soon be a howling tornado as it can be a gentle breeze that plays among the flowers. Because we can see Wind in the things it moves, be it leaves or hair, we often associate the Element of Air with the Wind. Yet air also has the capability of being still. Still Air is the invisible provider of life to our lungs. It should be noted that motionless Air can be the provider of gentle breath to our lungs but it can also stifle just as easy. Air can be oppressive, hot, and stifling just as easily as it can be cool and calming.

In this way, Air is influenced by Fire and Water for by Fire or Water can hair be heated or cooled.

There are many names for wind and every element in this book I want to share as simply as possible.

I had a vision once that if I close my mouth and nose for a while, I will almost forget all my visions and planning and focus on breathing. To remind ourselves not to take things for granted, let's take three long breaths and be grateful for the air and wind.

What if we had a temple of elements?

We need to find a way to reconnect to who we are and to is our source. Through connecting with the elements, of which we are part, we will find ultimate harmony.

The wind can be gentle and soothing to our senses, or destructive like a tornado.

Buddhist philosophy says everything is impermanent and changing, so we should be grateful for what we have now.

A few years ago, in California, there were severe wildfires. People had a hard time breathing and everyone had to wear masks while outside.

It took weeks for the air to clear.

Sometimes, it is only when something — like clean air — is lost, that we truly appreciate it.

Wind is our life force. We should never take for granted.

Lets together prayers to the wind.

Native American Prayer

Oh, Great Spirit
Whose voice I hear in the winds,
And whose breath gives life to all the world,
hear me, I am small and weak,
I need your strength and wisdom.
Let me walk in beauty and make my eyes ever behold
the red and purple sunset.
Make my hands respect the things you have
made and my ears sharp to hear your voice.
Make me wise so that I may understand the things
you have taught my people.
Let me learn the lessons you have
hidden in every leaf and rock.

I seek strength, not to be greater than my brother,
but to fight my greatest enemy - myself.
Make me always ready to come to you
with clean hands and straight eyes.
So when life fades, as the fading sunset,
my Spirit may come to you without shame.

(Translated by Lakota Sioux Chief Yellow Lark in 1887)
published in Native American Prayers - by the Episcopal
Church.

Fire Elements

The element that says we all come from somewhere is Fire, an that "somewhere" is the Sun. In Vajrayana Buddhism, the Sun is considered female energy because it is the very source of creation.

In Greek and Roman traditions, fire is one of the four classical elements. In ancient Greek philosophy and science it was commonly associated with the qualities of energy, assertiveness, and passion.

The first human that counseled anyone not to be play with fire was likely not a mother, but a shaman who knew well the beauty and fury of the fire elements.

From spiritual perspective fire represent our passion, compulsion, zeal, creativity and motivation.

The elements of fire has a great power of forging will and determination. It is our inner light as well as living symbol of divine fire that burns in every soul.

Like other Elements this means that fire has form in the earth plane and spiritual realms.

It is a source of energy that requires careful moderation or control or you will get burned or alternatively burn out.

Far Eastern philosophies see the fire as the forceful and primordial its physical manifestation is our metabolism . mentally it transeted into personal drive ,intention and desire.

One cannot help but think of early humans waving a fire in the air to send signal back and forth , as for immortality –our spirit is like a fingerprints we are of the stars and suns. we are of the fire..

When the elements of fire appear in the tarot it usually represent alchemical transformation or passion.

If you appear in a dream featuring fire and come out without burns it's a good sign that tumultuous times won't harm you.

Fire may also have connotation regarding purging and cleansing .

Fire Deities Nearly every Culture encountered has at least one, if not several, Deities that govern Fire and its vibration nature. Some easily recognizable ones include Agni, Astarte, Bast, Bel, Chango, Hephaestus; Hestia, Kali, Pele, Di Penates, Vulcan and Weland.

Let's pray together for the fire elements.

Universe, we thank you and give you praise for fire. We walk by fire's light.

through darkened times and places, fire illuminates each step along the path, even when the distant view is unclear and in shadow.

Fire purifies us, burning away the cluttered underbrush and making way for new growth to sprout forth from the ashes.

Fire warms and comforts us, dances for us, and energizes us.

In the process of this great transformation, we thank you for your present and gift to see us in the light.

To the fire element, we bow.

Earth Elements

The Element of Earth is substantive unlike the elusive Air element. When we think of Earth we can meditate on its beautiful and Healing Crystals & Stones, the soil in which we grow food, the plants and animals it sustains and even visualize it from space as a gentle reminder of our celestial Island.

Earth energies facilitate all manner of manifestation by putting down strong roots from which our dreams grow into reality. That is not to say that the Earth Element has nothing but positive characteristics. It can be fierce. Just watch a volcano erupt or the damage from a quake. This kind of power is why it is so important to respect our mother (you know the old saying: it's not nice to fool Mother Nature).

No matter where we are or what we do, the Earth is our teacher. When you sit on the ground, the Earth embraces you like a mother.

We need the Earth to help us connect with our deeper selves.

When we lack grounding, we lose our ability to think clearly.

When you sit on the ground in the garden take a couple of deep breaths, you can feel your root connecting with the Earth; you are in union with the Earth, and its healing, transformation, and alignment happens.

Have as much as awareness as possible that when you are sitting on the ground, you are part of the ground.

Today and every day, I treat Earth well and bless it in prayer.

An American Indian proverb reminds us to treat the Earth well because it is on loan to us from our children. The actions I take today will, in some way, affect the Earth and the future generations that will inhabit it, so I remain mindful of how I am treating the planet that is my home and sanctuary. And I bless the Earth in my prayers: "Universe, I thank you for Earth. With each step I take on its land and every stroke I swim in its waters, I treat my home well. With each breeze that caresses my face, I am reminded of the glory of this natural habitat. I pray that all inhabitants will be respectful of Earth and treat it well, making right decisions that will bless generations for years to come."

I do my part in being a caretaker of planet Earth.

When I look at the sky, hear the birds singing in the trees, or feel the heat of the sun on my face, I am reminded that planet Earth is a wonderful gift that the universe has given.

I am also reminded that I have an important responsibility as a caretaker of life on Earth.

I am thankful that plants take carbon dioxide from the air and give back life-sustaining oxygen. Lakes and rivers of the Earth provide the water needed for survival and recreation.

Refreshing rains replenish life in deserts, valleys, and plains. As a caretaker, I act in responsible, caring ways toward the environment. I do my part to ensure that the fruits of the Earth continue to flourish, the air remains pure, and the water supplies flow clean.

Space

Space is one of those vast things I don't know how to explain. I almost felt I should leave this page empty because any explanation is not enough.

Space is where we are all part of a macro-consciousness and our physical bodies exist as small structures within it. The universe contains a code to access the macro-consciousness and our bodies are a key that opens a portal or relationship with all other consciousnesses. Yoga, meditation, and chanting facilitate ways to connect with that the macro-consciousness of which we are part.

Space is always included in Thangka paintings It represents the vastness and possibilities of awakening and becoming.

Space is almost like our ultimate mother who holds everything. It is called Dharmakaya in Buddhism; a term meaning "the ultimate nature of everything," because it is space that allows everything to happen.

Every time I think of space I feel there are infinite possibilities. That is why it is good to go outside and see the sky, as much as possible. Look at the clear night sky and see the stars. Doing so reminds us that we are not alone in the vastness of the universe. We share this vast space with many other beings on the Earth and beyond it.

Every explanation of space is lacking because of its vastness, but know that when you breathe air and see sunsets and sunrises, that is the magic we experience in every breath.

Now, take a moment and breathe. Be grateful for all the elements and the space that are the magic of life.

Connecting back to the elements can be simple but also hard. Why hard? Because modern society often makes us separate from our otherwise natural connection to the elements and nature.

Many developed countries have progressed in many things, but we are still very far from connecting back to our hearts. I see vast possibilities in space for us to connect back to nature and find real harmony.

Let us open our hearts and minds to see the possibilities of connecting back to our macro-universe.

Mandala

There are many explanations and uses of mandalas in many countries and cultures. I would like to share what I understand about them, as an artist and practitioner.

What is the True Meaning and Importance of the Mandala?
The word "mandala," literally, means "circle." It represents infinite wholeness and is a cosmic diagram reminding us of our relationship to infinity, extending beyond and within our bodies and minds.

How to Use a Mandala
Mandalas have many meanings and uses, but the design of the mandala is meant to be so beautiful and aesthetically pleasing that it absorbs the mind in such a way that disturbing, irritating, or upsetting thoughts can't permeate the peaceful and spiritual essence surrounding the individual who is observing the mandala.

Gazing upon a visually pleasing mandala allows the observer

to tune into their higher levels of consciousness and awareness into an almost hypnotic state. We live in such a fast-paced world that it helps our chattering mind to slow down and be still while allowing our creative and spiritual side to run free.

In Buddhism, a mandala is a symbolic image of mind.

"Mind" here means all our mental abilities; all the space within our perception.

All the perceived Universe can be regarded as the contents of the mind, so a mandala can be called "the image of the Universe" as well.

A mandala is an object of concentration; therefore it usually depicts a clean mind — the Buddha's mind — to help us develop the qualities of a clean mind.

Therefore, a mandala in Buddhism depicts "Universe" or "Buddha's mind," or some particular aspects of Buddha's mind.

For example, there are images of enlightened beings, such as Bodhisattva Avalokiteshvara, embodiment of compassion; Bodhisattva Manjushri, embodiment of wisdom, and so on. These are images of aspects of the awakened mind and are used in practices that help one's mind tune-in to the same qualities.

Micro to Macro

Representing the universe itself, a mandala is both the microcosm and the macrocosm, and we are all part of its intricate design. The mandala is more than an image seen with our eyes; it is an actual moment in time. It can be can be used as a vehicle to explore art, science, religion and life itself. The mandala contains an encyclopedia of the finite and a road map to infinity.

Carl Jung said that a mandala symbolizes "a safe refuge of inner reconciliation and wholeness." It is "a synthesis of distinctive elements in a unified scheme representing the basic nature of existence." Jung used the mandala for his own personal growth and wrote about his experiences.

Different Cultures, Similar Expressions

Both from Navajo Nation of First Nation people and Hi-amlayan Buddhist monks create **sand mandalas** to demonstrate the impermanence of life

In ancient Himalayas as part of a spiritual practice, monks created intricate mandalas with colored sand powder.

The tradition still continues to this day as the Buddhist monks travel to different countries around the world to create sand mandalas and educate people about the culture and teachings of Hiamalyas

The creation of a sand mandala requires many days to complete. Each mandala contains many religious symbols that must be perfectly reproduced each time the mandala is created.

When finished, the monks gather in a colorful ceremony, chanting in deep tones as they sweep their mandala into a jar and empty it into a nearby body of water as a blessing. This action also symbolizes symbolizes the cycle of life.

A world away, the First Nation Navajo people also create impermanent sand paintings which are used in spiritual rituals–in much the same way as they are used by Himalayan Monks. A Navajo sandpainting ritual may last from five to nine days and range in size from three to fifteen feet or more.

Planet Earth is a Mandala

As these previous descriptions of the mandala explain, they are sacred, just as the Earth is sacred.

When I look at modern life, I see how we can be so filled with ego, saying things like, "I can do anything I want to the Earth." Yet while we often take it for granted, I have seen people change their attitudes when they become older and wiser, realizing the importance of the eco-system rather then "ego-system."

Many things try to separate us from harmony. We say we belong to this political party or that club; to this religion or that organization. I belong to nature's family.   The ego-driven mentality is strong, but when something suddenly happens to break its hold on us, we see the eco-system clearly.

Sometimes, we experience dark times in life that ultimately teach us to value and understand the light and wisdom.

In my own life experience, I needed to learn is to be patient and have more discipline to better see reality. I am sure what I understand as realty may be different from your perspective, but as far as the reality of the elements are concerned, we do not have to agree or disagree—they are absolute truth.

No matter where we are or what our cultural or spiritual practice, we are in a fundamental union with the elements and that's the truth—and it's what we want to re-connect with to find harmony.

Mandala also means harmony. It is one of the great examples where we can see the structure and union of the elements of Earth and remember that harmony.

Some unhealthy spiritual leaders and unhealthy political leaders try to cause disharmony between brotherhood and sisterhood, and take advantage of others. One must beware of these false prophets.

Our life is a journey where we seek the light of wisdom. It can be found when we spend more time in the nature.

There is a fictionalized picture of the Earth from space that shows our planet to be breathing that illustrates that the Earth is a living thing that we need to live with in harmony. Before we find harmony outside it is important to discover harmony within. The practice of breathing and hugging trees can be beneficial and useful as a way to develop this harmony.

Spiritual Life

Spirituali In general, it includes a sense of connection to something bigger and higher than ourselves, and it typically involves a search for meaning in life. As such, it is a universal human experience—something that touches us all In our deeper level .

Life is an interesting, diverse journey and we choose in life the things we want to keep or release. One's spiritual life is different for everyone. Some follow one practice, while others follow another. In our spiritual life, we ought to see each other with kindness and without judgment or anger, because when we have anger or hatred towards others, we are not fully living a spiritual life .

How can we make our spiritual life meaningful?

The answer is simple. When we pray or meditate, we ought to include all sentient beings in our prayers. When you help others, help as many as possible. Do not judge the spiritual practices of others. Develop as much as compassion as possible for everyone.

At this moment, I am writing as I sit in my gallery in downtown Berkeley, California. Life is not normal here, as something is happening all the time. I see people screaming and going crazy in the street, sleeping on sidewalks, and asking for money and food.

In life, we will always have plenty of opportunities to practice compassion and love, whether towards others or oneself.

Meditation Practice with Elements

Now let's practice some meditation with elements.

Take a few deep breaths and relax the body.

Let us remember our parents for their kindness for giving birth.

Let us be grateful for the Sun and Moon, and all the elements fire, water, earth, wind, and space,

Let us be thankful and take three deep breaths with each element.

Three long breaths for fire as we remember fire as a significant transformational element.

Let us be thankful for the wind for movement, water for life, earth for grounding, and space, which contains everything.

With each breath, we become filled with gratitude for each element.

Now, let us visualize our veins traveling down into the earth, like roots seeking nourishment. Visualize the blood in your veins descending into the soil, reconnecting with all the elements.

Be still and calm in that posture; relax your breath and let each breath fill with gratitude so that you are now reconnecting to your roots.

Stay like that for 15 to 25 minutes, then pray that we may all be reconnected with our roots and the elements.

Slowly open your eyes and look around. Be grateful in your heart and remember: The key to joy in life is to have gratitude in one's heart.

The Benefit of Hugging Trees

Modern society creates a lot of stress in our lives, which is why more and more people are turning to the gifts of nature for therapy, like tree-hugging. Though many still associate tree-hugging with a hippy lifestyle, hugging a tree can be good for your health.

According to the book, *Blinded by Science* by Matthew Silverstone, there is evidence that trees provide health benefits for mental illnesses such as Attention Deficit Hyperactivity Disorder and depression. Children function better cognitively and emotionally when they interact with plants. Although many believe it's the green open spaces that contribute to the effect, Silverstone demonstrates that the vibrational properties of trees and plants offer health benefits. An article in *Natural News* indicates that if you drink a glass of water treated with a 10HZ vibration, your blood coagulation rates will change immediately on ingesting the treated water.

Hugging a tree increases levels of the hormone oxytocin. This hormone is responsible for feeling calm and emotional bonding. When hugging a tree, the hormones serotonin and dopamine make you feel happier. It is important to use this "free" space of a forest we were given by nature to holistically heal ourselves.

Forest Bathing

I have almost spend everyday of my life in California walking to hills and sitting under the tree and I found this is very essence to many cultural including Japanese cultural and science have proven that it helps in many different level including enhance the immune system.

By taking stroll in the forest, it can make you healthier.

The smell of woods and the wind it create some kind of healing elements that helps us to fight our sickness.

Talk to Trees

Trees are the best counselors because they're good at listening, quiet, trustworthy, and entirely at your service for free. Talking to a tree helps you feel not judged, creates mental clarity and emotional cleansing, causing you to feel lighter and happier.

Talk to Yourself

Today, society looks down and portrays people as crazy if they talk to themselves. However, there are many benefits to this crazy practice. The forest can be a place where you can completely feel in touch with yourself and speak as freely as you want. So next time you want to take a stroll in the forest, don't forget to shout, cry, laugh, and feel all at the same time!

The True Meaning of Beauty

There is more to beauty than what we see on the outside, like a new car or house. Beauty and perfection are ideas in the mind.

We might see a structure and think it perfect or beautiful and can also see beauty in the forest where there are so many different kinds of plants. When you walk in the street and see different types of people, that too is beautiful.

The inspiration for this writing about beauty came from walking in the street where I saw a woman with a severely burned face. She was looking at me and I found myself judging her. I thought, "Who am I to judge her? Why do we judge?"

When we see others with our hearts, we see the soul. We see life.

"Namaste" means "I bow to you." There is deep meaning and symbolism associated to this simple act of folding the hands and bowing the head. It also means:

My soul honors your soul.

I honor the place in you where the entire universe resides. I honor the light, love, truth, beauty, and peace within you, because it also within me.

I sharing these things we are united, we are the same, we are one.

At the mental level, namaste is the total surrender - dropping of the I - and accepting the Supreme Truth in all animate and inanimate. It is merging with the Universal Truth.

The coming of the palms together is again very special symbol. Due to maya (illusion) we believe that there is the other. But reality there is no second - all that is here is supreme truth. By bringing together palms we are indicating that there is only One - everything rises and sets in that single One.

The real beauty is when we honor each other and one of the fundamental things we got lost of understanding the meaning of beauty is because of we got lost from connection of elements,

I encourage everyone reading this book to spend as much time as possible in nature to reconnect with the elements.

Some notions of beauty are colored by expectations or illusions. We can see past these illusions by hugging trees and being in nature.

We all desire clarity of oneness so we try religion or follow some philosophy. But it does not need to be so complicated. By connecting with the elements we can find that real meaning of oneness, and through that we can have harmony within and out.

The Real Meaning of Success

While everyone desires success, sometimes we don't consider what success really is. In Western societies, it is generally associated with materialism—the more things one owns, and the "better" or more expensive those things are, the more successful one is. But is that really success?

I feel most successful when I am at peace with myself and others; when I am connected with the world in a positive way, and feel satisfied and joyous about life.

In my experience, if I tend to place too much importance on material possessions, the flow of harmony in my life is disturbed, and I no longer feel as "successful" as I do when I focus upon inner peace and living in harmony with others and the world around me.

We all learn through our mistakes and at some point in life we realize that the happiness or inner peace we seek has always been there with us, like a shadow that is never separated from us.

So what blocks our inner happiness? Because we learn in childhood that external things bring happiness, we may never have the chance to connect with our inner self, which is where true happiness and "success" resides. To make matters worse, because parents are often busy, many children turn to technology—computers, phones, and video games—seeking happiness, only to end up being confused about notions and ideas about happiness and success.

A man once told me, while his parents worked so hard to buy him toys and other things, it never made him truly happy; what he really wanted was to spend more time with his parents.

Many parents seem to believe that spending more time working to earn money to buy things will make their children happy, but as this man's story explains, that isn't the case. It's okay to work hard, but for children to be truly happy and to have a "successful," family life, spending more time together is of more value. child .

Today, as a father himself, that man works less so that he can spend more time with his daughter, and both he and his daughter are happier because of it.

As Buddha explained, "Money is never going to make you ultimately happy."

Success in life is having inner balance, a happy family, and remembering why you are here on Earth. This kind of success brings inner peace and balance, whereas having only money can be a fundamental cause of stress.

There is no path to happiness. Happiness *is* the path. Do not wait to become happy; take a deep breath and recognize that being happy is already within, if you are grateful to be alive. That gratitude will lead you to inner peace.

The Meaning of Spirituality

For some, spirituality is just another fashionable trend that people follow to be "cool."

I sometimes see people walking along the street with their yoga mats, for example, who probably have little knowledge about yoga as something other than exercise.

Spirituality has many branches, and there are many different traditions and belief systems within it.

Someone reading this certainly might know more than I do about it, so all I can do is speak about it from my perspective and experience.

Having traveled to a few countries I have been exposed to many spiritual traditions and practices. What I find interesting is that each person's practice is true for them, yet they are all similar in that they have a base of the same characteristics.

Spirituality involves finding one's own path while also discovering that path's similarities with others, much like different rivers that all flow to the same ocean.

And when I practice Vajrayan Buddhism, I am also open to practice with the elements. I can talk and have tea with brothers and sisters around the world and we can all speak about shared beliefs and how we intend to take care of the elements for future generations.

The more and more I practice elemental spirituality, the more I feel that I am sharing basic spiritual principles with the broader community.

This world is diverse, with countless traditions, practices, and belief systems. That diversity is beautiful, and we should honor it.

We are all one—that is our ultimate nature—but we appear in this world at different levels and in different places, with different cultures.

Some people believe there is one god, some believe there is none, and some believe in many gods and goddesses. Regardless of your beliefs,

let's put aside our differences and agree to have a simple conversation about the elements—the trees, rivers, and clouds.

Every element has a scientific name and explanation, but there is no limitation on space and time or how everything works.

That's why the magic happens every day; we only need to be open to see it.

Our minds often block the magic, but if they can be unrestricted, we can see the magic happening in everything.

When I am sitting next to a river listening to it flow, feeling the wind, I feel blessed by the elements.

My Native American Flute Offering

I am drawn to wind instruments.

I love the sound when I play and think, "Wow, the wind can make beautiful sounds."

And it's not only the instrument that makes sound but my breathing too.

I once did try playing the Nepali Bansuri Flute when I was a boy.

I loved it but somehow did not feel connected. I used to play it in the evening when it was calm and quiet. I played almost every evening on the roof when I was in Kathmandu, looking at the Swayambhunath temple. My playing was an offering to the temple.

When I came to the United States, I was pulled by the energy of Native American culture. I am grateful for that energy that led me to the flute.

Playing it touches my soul and connects with and aligns my spirit.

The first flute I played is made of California Redwood.

I have been playing for a few years and feel amazed and blessed whenever I play. Playing is like offering medicine to a sick world. I enjoy playing so much that I even produced and released an album entitled *Honoring the Land*.

Today I own thirteen flutes and hope to collect more of them as a part of my offering to the instrument I am so passionate about.

Music and art are medicines I am offering to the world right now, and I feel grateful and satisfied by giving it.

When I play the Native American flute it is not just a flute I am playing; I am honoring and respecting Native American culture.

I am from Nepal, but when I am playing the Native American flute, I feel grateful that I am connected with "flute medicine." I then take that medicine and offer it as music to the world.

I am interested in breathing meditation, and yoga called *prana yoga*, where one uses breathing to relax and awaken the body's energy. Likewise, I am drawn to flute playing, which involves the same breathing techniques, although for making melodic sounds.

May I continue offering the sound for the benefit of all.

Finding Natural Unfolding

Nature unfolding is very important. We all try many things in life, but if what we do does not come from a natural place, there is going to be a lot of pressure.

Consider the concept of Yin and Yang, or black and white, or what Native Americans call black wolf and white wolf.

In my practice, whether painting, playing the flute, or meditating, I work on how I can balance both things and find the natural balance or unfolding.

We all go through many challenges in life, but finding balance, natural law, and natural unfolding, are the keys to not being frustrated at the end of the day.

Whenever I see natural phenomena, like a full moon, a solar eclipse, or a river flowing, I am amazed at the beauty and balance.

Human beings do many things to try and make life easier and better, but do these things really work? Is life becoming better? The answer is found in how we are using what we have made.

Talking about the future does not mean we forget what we want right now, and natural unfolding in life is allowing yourself to do what you can right now, for yourself and others. If we want to help others, we must help ourselves first. Like in a plane, where we learn to put on our oxygen mask first, then help others put on their masks.

Science and ancient yoga practices both confirm that if you do not find the natural way of releasing the emotions, harmful hormones are released into one's body. So finding a natural release, whether by dancing, singing, or hugging trees, is what we must do to release our emotions.

For example, I like walking in nature and finding a place to sit. I slowly inhale and exhale, while keeping compassion in my heart.

When we do deep breathing like this, we are expanding our lungs and creating healthy circulation for the heart,

Nothing in life is certain. I remember hearing about a great Buddhist teacher named 16th Karmapa who died at the age of 57. Even at that young age, he died as a spiritual leader or teacher. Sometimes, even great teachers only live a short time, but what is most important in life is to find a way to live each day fully.

One of the real quality things about the great teachers is they live life every day, fully, and that is the practice should emulate. Discovering the natural unfolding and learning and understating about life is important.

Just like when we feel hungry, we cook food or go out to eat, we need to learn what is best.

Make Every Day Special

I would like to share a quote from 8th century Master Guru Padmasambhava:

If you want to know your past, look at your present condition.

If you want to know your future, look at your present action.

Many times, we do not value daily life but think only about the future.

While it is the mind's job to think, we need to add to our thinking the awareness of our every action. The point is, how do we make every day extraordinary?

I like to start my morning by taking a moment to breathe deeply, honoring the land. I am grateful for all my teachers, my parents, and the elements. After I do this, I meditate, do some chanting, and go for a walk.

It's very good and important to have a little moment for yourself in the morning, especially if you live in a city where life is busy. To have a moment of reflection and awareness for oneself is the best way to start the day and make every day special.

In Buddhism and Hinduism, light symbolizes changing the darkness of ignorance into luminous wisdom, so I also turn on a light and focus my attention upon it. Often, in Buddhist temples (mostly in Himalayan Buddhism) you will find many oil lamps burning.

There are many reasons Buddhists burn oil lamps. They do it for people who have passed away, for new births, for sending wishes, to express gratitude to Buddha, and to recognize the Buddha nature within.

In this fast-moving world, to experience everyday spirituality is difficult, so for that reason, many go to retreats. In my experience, retreats are great because it is a good way to take care of yourself. It is also important to make every day meaningful and spiritual.

I have a gallery of sacred art in Berkeley, California, that I am closing at the end of 2019 so that I can go on a retreat. The whole intention to have a gallery and share my paintings with the world was and is to share that we can all have a sacred space in our house and make every day spiritually special.

Thangka paintings are also called "scroll paintings," because they can be rolled-up, making them easy to take from one place to another.

Sometimes, we think spiritual is only when we go to a temple or read this text and that text, but to make everyday spiritual, we have to understand the temple is within; we must connect with the divine within.

While going to the temple on a certain day and time is fine, the best time to practice the spiritual is this moment.

Let your mind not be confused thinking about making a spiritual life in the future. It is embodied at this moment.

Breathe in.

Take a deep breath.

Be grateful for the elements.

Open your heart let the light enter. Reconnect yourself and recognize you are the light.

Collective Awakening

Collective consciousness-awakening is happening around the world. Because of the internet, we are more connected.

Many things can be used for more than one purpose. In esoteric Buddhist practices, for example, poison is transformed into medicine, and anger into wisdom.

In this age of awakening, we are fortune to have access to ways of connecting with people around the world.

This enlightenment or awakening does not mean we have all the same traditions or practices; it means each person can find a path that is right for them, and develop an understanding of oneness.

We make Mandela paintings, but we also paint many other deities and symbols that represent collective awakening.

"Bodhisattva" is a Sanskrit name for the saintly being's who are constantly working to help people understand themselves.

We should support, in whatever way possible, people who

are helping animals and Mother Nature. We all share planet Earth, and as brothers and sisters, we need to learn to live in harmony and help each other. We are all on our journey of awakening and remembering who we are,

We are all light beings, and what blocks the light is our separation from nature. I now see people re-connecting back to self and nature. Creating sounds with various ancient instruments, and sacred chanting, helps people re-connect.

In my gallery, here in Berkeley, I have hosted more than 200 events, where everyone is joyful by re-connecting.

Collective awakening in this 21st century age is our only option. There is no other choice to shift our consciousness to what is most important, to shape the present back into alignment with nature.

Guru Padmasambhava

Guru Padmasambhava was a 7th century Master known for his ability to transform all phenomena into Dharma. He was a great Buddhist teacher and shaman.

He looks different from other deities, and it is said that he conducted most of his practices in cemeteries and charnel ground.

Guru Padmasambhava's life is still a mystery for many, and the way to connect with him is visiting places where he meditated. The fascinating thing about guru Padmasambhava is that he was a friend to all good shamans.

One of the great stories I remember reading is when Guru Padmasambhava, the king, and abbot Santaraksita, built a temple in Tibet. Before Padmasambhava traveled to Tibet, he meditated in a cave in Nepal.

Santaraksita was an abbot of a great university and monastery. He was invited to Tibet to build a temple, but the spirits did not allow it. He would build in the day, but at night, the spirits would come and take it down.

Then, the people heard about a great master, Padmasambahva, who was also known as Guru Rinpoche to the Himalayan people. He was known as a great shamanic teacher and tantric master at that time.

When he came to Tibet, people did not believe him because he looked like a crazy guy.

The way Tibet's first temple, called Samye monastery, was built, began when Guru Padmasamvhava visited the site. He sat and did some mantras and rituals, and invited all the spirits to enjoy food and drinks. The spirits became so happy, they helped build it in the night. That is how the temple was built in such a short amount of time. This is how the Buddha Dharma teachings were established in Tibet.

The moral of this story is that Padmasambhava was able to bring harmony, even for sprits, by honoring and remembering them.

We must remember our ancestors and honor the land if we want to build somewhere.

Berkeley, California, used to be the land of the Ohlone people. This tribe treated the land as being sacred, but today there is a shopping mall where there was once sacred land and a Native American cemetery.

This kind of thing happens in many places and in many countries. Hopefully, by reading about this, you will want value and honor the land.

The best way to create a better life is by learning from indigenous peoples and about nature and the elements, then sharing what we learn with our children, because they are our future.

If you search online for Guru Padmasambhava, you will find many stories about him, and you will learn about his teachings. According to the Guru, the most important teaching is to connect with your body, speech, and mind.

In Buddhism, our actions in life are created through three doors. 1) *Body*, which means doing things with our body; 2) *Speech*, which means we create negative or positive actions through talking; and 3) *Thought*, whereby our thinking, we create positive and negative.

When we try our best to be aware of these three doors, which we are constantly doing, something inside, at our deepest level, will help us connect to ourselves. .

Mind Essence ~ Padmasambhava

Where the past has ceased and the future has not yet arisen,
In the unimpeded state of present wakefulness,
Rest in the manner of mind looking into mind.
No matter what thoughts may arise at this time,
They are all the display of the single mind essence.
As the nature of space is unchanging,
You will realize the all-pervasive mind essence to be changeless.
This is the Great Perfection, the ultimate of all vehicles,
The unexcelled meaning of the self-existing Mind Section.

Be Grateful for What you Have

Being grateful for what we have is one way to find peace in life. In this fast-moving, modern world, we are constantly looking outside and keep buying things to try and fulfill our needs. But are we happy?

More isn't necessarily better. When we see advertisements suggesting that if we buy this or eat that we'll be happy, we should remember that buying things doesn't bring true happiness.

I often encounter homeless people who were once rich or well-known. These people were often praised because of their status, but now that they are weak or poor, they are treated like "nobodies."

In Buddhism this is what is called the "cycle of life." We are poor, then we become rich, then poor again. We are a billionaire one day, then the very next day, we become homeless.

Being grateful for what we have will always increase the level of inner peace because what we are seeking is already within us, like a shadow that is never apart from us.

It took me some time to realize that.

Being grateful is essential to a happy life. An excellent place to start, for example, is being thankful for our parents.

Be grateful that you were born where the teachings of enlightened masters are still available.

Be grateful that we can connect with like-minded people.

Be grateful for breathing.

Be grateful we have the power to change our lives.

Be grateful for all the teachers of every tradition, who are working to benefit everyone.

Be grateful to be alive and to be awake.

Let's take a moment to remember the kindness of our parents, for taking care of us when we were children.

The kindness of our parents is unconditional love. If we want to know the meaning of unconditional love, we can remember our parents.

When we feel grateful, even for our enemies, we open our hearts with unconditional love.

The ultimate nature of human consciousness is unconditional love, as written about in many holy texts.

If one's heart and mind are blocked with unhealthy emotions, and we need to find a way to transform those emotions. We need to find a way to recognize those emotions, then change them.

The cause of suffering in life is love with boundaries and dualistic thoughts.

We all have an opportunity to reconnect back to our true

nature of mind by walking in nature and being in the forest. This removes blocks and opens the mind.

I hope to create a space called "temple of elements," in my homeland of Nepal, to help people connect back to the elements and remove their blockages.

Shamans around the world are able to remove the blockages, so the place I am building will include a space for shamans to perform their rituals and ceremonies.

Being grateful for the elements is fundamental for achieving alignment with them.

Society may label you, but nature has the answer that we can each remember by connecting back to nature.

If your parents are alive, call them and say, "I love you," and, "thank you."

And if your parents have passed away, even if you had rough childhood, take a moment to remember them, and be grateful. Whether they are good or bad does not matter.

Yoga practitioners and scientists have found that when we feel grateful, in heart and mind, we produce a healing hormone that can heal 90% of diseases and illnesses.

Lotus Meditation

There are many ways to meditate. Here I will share with you the lotus flower technique.

The lotus flower is an old and significant symbol in many religions, especially Hinduism and Buddhism. While there are slight variations to the lotus flower meaning in the different faiths, the general concept is the same.

The meaning of the lotus flower comes from the way the flower grows in nature. It starts off as a bud underwater, often in murky ponds, and grows until it emerges from the muddy waters in a beautiful blooming flower.

Symbol for Spiritual Enlightenment: The meaning of the lotus flower symbol comes from an analogy derived from the flower's life cycle, where all humans are born into a world of suffering where they must learn to overcome difficult times so that they can become a better person and reach enlightenment.

The muddy waters represent the struggles of life, the bud of the flower represent a person that has not yet reached their full potential, and the blossoming lotus flower above the water represents someone who has achieved nirvana or enlightenment and let go of worldly suffering.

Symbol for Purity: The lotus flower emerges from dirty waters perfectly clean and beautiful, so it is also a symbol of purity.

The meaning of the lotus flower holds such power because it can offer hope and strength to the people struggling in their daily lives.

It is a symbol that shows that no matter where you start off in life and no matter what you're going through, you have the ability to rise above, overcome all negativity and find bliss as you emerge from your struggles.

Symbol of Personal Progress: The physical aspects of the lotus flower have also contributed to its meaning. The lotus flower has many petals that surround the center in multiple concentric layers. As the petals open, more petals are revealed until the lotus is in full bloom and all the layers are revealed. This process is seen as a metaphor for the progress made in gradual stages to ultimately reach spiritual enlightenment and self-realization.

HISTORY OF THE LOTUS
FLOWER IN ANCIENT EGYPT

While it's difficult to trace back the earliest depictions of the lotus flower, its use has been dated back to Ancient Egypt. The lotus flower was known as "Seshen" in Egypt and was actually cultivated in ponds. Due to its significant meaning and association with their gods, it was believed that the lotus flower offered strength and power.

The Ancient Egyptians also believed in the lotus flower as a symbol of rebirth as it closed its petals at night and would bloom again in the morning. This was believed to symbolize the process where the dead would enter the underworld to be reborn.

Symbol of lotus flower in Buddhsim

THE MEANING OF LOTUS FLOWRE IS VERY ESSANCE TO BUDDHISM BECAUSE IT IS A SYMBOL OF PURITY AND ALSO SYMBLOIZE EVERYONE CAN BECOME BUDDHA.

THE FLOWER GROWS FROM THE MUD AND BUT NEVER GET EFFECTED BY THE MUD AND THAT'S THE SYMBOL OF OUR TRANSFROMATION AND A JOURNEY OF ENLIGHTENMENT.

In Buddhism, the lotus flower symbolizes purity and transformation of the mind, body and spirit, as the flower, or soul, blossoms above and moves freely over dirty waters, which represents the struggles of life, attachment and desire.

The flower also symbolizes detachment as water rolls off the petals easily, meaning that the transformation or awakening of the soul.

Let's meditate on that:

Sit comfortably, either in a chair or on a cushion, or even lie down.

Take a few deep, relaxing breaths and try to focus on breathing.

Keep gratitude in your heart for Mother Earth holding us.

Now, imagine the lower part of your body, below the belly, as being the realm of dirty water.

Let's now imagine that lower part as the realm of lust, greed, and desire, and all the emotions that are not needed; but still keep gratitude in your heart for even those disturbing emotions.

Now imagine your spinal cord as a lotus trunk, rising from all the emotions.

Imagine your head as a lotus flower, being deeply connected to the ground through a root, which is all that emotion.

With every breath, you are opening your lotus petals.

Now connect with your heart. Take few deep, relaxing breaths, and feel your heart.

In this meditation, we are connecting the mind and heart with all the emotions.

With relaxed breathing, stay focused on your breathing and imagine your lotus mind connecting to your heart, as they become one.

Remain in that connected zone for about 5 to 10 minutes, through your breathing.

Finally, dedicate this meditation on the oneness and connection of mind and heart, to all sentient beings.

14) With this, we end this meditation.

You can practice this meditation in the morning or evening, or any time, wherever you'd like.

We are all evolving and becoming lotus flowers!

In this journey of becoming, I hope we can all connect within ourselves and become like lotus flowers.

While doing this meditation, if you want to listen to my music, search for "Honoring The Land By Anil Thapa," online and you will find it. May my music be beneficial for your meditation journey.

Meditation on Gazing Practice

Gazing practice is one of the fundamental practices in Buddhism that helps us to connect within.

Normally, you use certain images and gaze at different enlightened masters.

It helps to remember who we are because in Buddhism, there is no difference between an enlightened master and you—we simply don't recognize our true nature.

Certain mantras are used to create vibrations that help us journey deep within.

Now I will share with you how to use nature for gazing practice:

Sit on a chair or cushion, or just on the floor—wherever you are comfortable.

Take a few long, relaxing breaths and connect with your heart.

Make sure your spine is straight and open your eyes halfway.

Whenever you meditate, make sure your back is straight.

Now gaze at a mountain, at trees, a river, or grass; something in nature for 10 to 15 minutes.

When you are done gazing, close your eyes and feel the object inside. If you were gazing at water, feel it. If you were gazing at a tree, feel it inside.

Contemplate upon the idea that you are part of those elements—that you are those elements.

Relax with your eyes closed for 5 to 10 minutes and feel the connection.

You can practice this anytime you want.

After you are in a state of oneness with the elements, dedicate the energy of oneness to all sentient beings.

End your session with peace and gratitude for the elements.

Yab Yum (Divine Union)

Yab Yum is also called father and mother, and in Buddhism, mostly in Himalayan Buddhism, you will see pictures of masculine and feminine energy joining together.

Sometimes, people are a little confused about this.

What is Buddha doing—having sex?

First, we have to understand that this image symbolizes the masculine and feminine energy within ourselves. The images are naked because that is our ultimate nature of mind or consciousness.

In Himalayan Buddhism, we use these images as a visualization practice, to find the harmony within and to remember that we have these two energies within.

Samantabhadra is the primordial Buddha associated with compassion, known as a protector of the sutra. Samantabhadra is the antecedent of all and the expanse of reality. Samantabhadra is blue in color, symbolizing the empty essence of the mind, and Samantabhadri is white in color, symbolizing the clear, knowing aspect of the mind.

The unity of emptiness and the cognizant aspect of being is thus depicted as the male and female form of Adi-Buddha. Adi-Buddha never meant first Buddha or creator of the Universe.

In Tantra, the Earth is the divine feminine force—Mother Earth—and the Heavens are the divine, masculine force—Father Sky.

Any seasoned meditator will tell you that meditating lying down is not the same as sitting upright. Enlightenment always happens while one is in a vertical position, hence other statues of deities will most often be in a sitting pose. So Yab-Yum, often thought of as a love-making posture, is actually the ultimate posture for tantric meditation.

Milarepa

Deep in the wild mountains, there is a strange marketplace, where you can trade the hassle and noise of everyday life, for eternal Light.

Jetsun Milarepa was a Tibetan siddha. He was a murderer as a young man but then turned to Buddhism to become an accomplished buddha, despite his past.

Milarepa is one of those yogis who will be remembered. He was one of the great examples that show transformation is possible.

Milarepa is remembered for his remarkable determination and personal growth. His inspiring story traces the very familiar, human progression from confusion to clarity. Early in his life, Milarepa came to understand tenents of both privilege and oppression. Though born to a wealthy family, the death of Milarepa's father left him and his mother at the mercy of his aunt and uncle, who put them to work as servants for their own family. At his mother's request, Milarepa studied the craft of black magic to retaliate against their cruelty. Not only was he successful in mastering these magical abilities, he promptly used his skills to take the lives of his aunt and uncle's entire family. In this way, Milarepa had invited an immense amount of negative karma into his life as a young adult. Soon after committing these crimes, Milarepa's joy at having aided his mother began to fade, making way for inescapable remorse. This transformation led Milarepa to seek out a master teacher.

Milarepa a great yogi have touched the hearts of many students near and far .His life represent a noble Bodhisattva, as his deep love and compassion created wish of bodhichitta and the motivation him to obtain the Buddhahood for the benefit of all sentient beings .

Four Noble Truths in Buddhism

What are the four noble truths?
Buddhism's teaching has many different layers.

The four noble truths are what we called the "fundamental truths'" and everything evolves from them.

Everything in life has its causes and conditions. Sometimes we understand them, and sometimes we don't.

To learn about the connections in life and how every act creates a ripple effect is what we call "the art of living."

1. Suffering
The very fundamental truth of life is it includes many ups and down.We are constantly busy fulfilling ourself with external things and trying to make ourself happy. No matter what we do we can not escape from suffering of old age suffering of sikness and suffering of death .

2. The Cause of Suffering
The very cause of suffering is ignorance and the idea of self and ego of I

The very cause of suffering is I and making separation from others . Ego which constaly build its like a identity of separation and because of that we are always separated of our true nature which is one with everything .

3. The End of Suffering
The good news is that we can end our suffering or we can

transform them into bliss. we have to recognize that everything's in life is temporarily including suffering.

Everything in life is like a passing clouds in the sky ,for example the clouds appear in the sky and stay sometime and despair. everything is in journey of transformation we have to suffering can end because we can all transform our obscurations

4. The Path

By living mindfully, practicing meditation-developing wisdom, we can all take exactly the same journey to enlightenment and freedom from illusion ,We can to awaken to our true nature of mind . like Buddha did.

Honoring the Land and Alignment with the Elements is intended to embody, in every day and in whatever way possible, the last truth of Buddhist philosophy; to explain how by living ethically and practicing meditation, we can all find the path to reconnect to ourselves.

Thangka Art and Human Consciousness

One of my inspirations for writing this book and playing Native American flute, came from this art that I am sharing around the world.

I shared a few things already about Thangka paintings, and I will now share a little more detail about Thangka Art.

For me, Thangka Art has always been a way to understand the world and how it works. It also helps me understand more about myself.

The deities shown in Thangka paintings are usually depictions of visions that appeared to great spiritual masters at moments of realization, that were then recorded and incorporated into Buddhist scripture. The proportions are considered sacred as not only are they exact representations of Buddhist deities, but also the visual expression of spiritual realizations that occurred at the time of a vision.

Thangka painting is thus a two-dimensional medium illustrating a multi-dimensional spiritual reality.

Practitioners use Thangkas as a sort of road map to guide them to the original insight of the master. This map must be accurate and it is the responsibility of the artist to make sure it is so in order for a Tthangka to be considered genuine, or to be useful as a support for Buddhist practice, guiding one to the proper place.

The reason I say human consciousness is because Thangka reflects the ultimate or relative nature of the mind. In most of the Thangka paintings you will also find many hills, clouds, and mountains, also to depict the notion that we are not separated from the elements.

Buddha-nature is never separated from the elements. If we want to have peace, become happy, or want to become enlightened, we must make elements our base and be grateful.

Human consciousness has different appearances because we all grow up in different places. We eat different food and wear different clothes because we all think differently.

In Thangka Art, there are sometimes peaceful scenes and sometimes wrathful ones. Sometimes they include abstract circle paintings that symbolize our consciousness in different perspectives.

In the Vajrayana Tantric Buddhist practice, many images are used for what we call "the guru yoga practice." In this, we use specific images to understand teachers and gurus, and by visualizing images, we can understand that we have those qualities already inside.

Vajrayana Buddhism is almost like a practice of alchemy whereby we practice transforming our minds and thoughts into Buddha-nature, by using enlightened images from Thangka.

As long as Thangka Art is in existence, we will have many possibilities to connect with our nature of mind, which is Buddha-nature, or enlightenment nature.

The reason we use Thangka paintings is that our nature of mind is being covered with many relative emotions, which are all part of everything. But those relative emotions are like drinking saltwater, which will never fulfill the thirsty.

How do we use Thangka in Meditation?

Sit comfortably and concentrate on an image. Practice gazing for a time—maybe five to ten minutes. If you have a certain mantra, chant it as you are gazing.

After this, slowly close your eyes and relax.

Can you see the image in your mind when you close your eyes?

If you can see the image, bring the awareness to your heart and dedicate that energy to all sentient beings.

If you cannot see the image after gazing, or if it's blurry, keep gazing until you see the image clearly inside yourself.

This is one way to train the mind so that it won't wander here and there; to focus and relax.

Thangka paintings are the visual expression of an awakened state of enlightenment—this being the ultimate goal of the Buddhist spiritual path. That's why a Thangka is sometimes called,

"The roadmap to enlightenment."

The very act of creating Thangka is a sacred art; a form of religious Sadhana or meditation. Thangka Art is thus placed in monasteries and temples, where they are profoundly respected as objects of devotion and meditation. It is thus imperative for us to not only preserve the Thangka, but also to keep the glorious artistic tradition of past intact for the years to come.

The Benefit of Walking Barefoot and Sitting Under a Tree

Walking barefoot was always something I enjoyed as a child.

There is something about nature—it is a "mega university"—where many things we feel, like walking barefoot, are important in life.

When we needed shoes, we built many different kinds, with different brands.

Now we have gone so far that we need science to explain why walking barefoot is good. We lost our connection with nature and need reasons to connect back.

It almost feels unnatural now to live in harmony with nature.

More and more, people in science and healthcare understand the benefits of walking barefoot in nature.

It turns out the sensation we feel when we walk bare feet it is more then just a feeling.

This Treapeutic touch of Mother Nature is resulting remarkable benefits for mind and body.

Mental Balance

Healthy Blood Flow

Improving sleeping

Reduce many sickness of the body.

The primordial practice of walking barefoot, sometimes referred to as "grounding," is only just beginning to be studied by modern science. One of the most groundbreaking findings is the powerful *heart health* effect of direct skin contact with the earth.

Sitting under a Tree

I have been fortunate these last six years as there are many trees here in Berkeley, California.

I walk in nature almost every day, and sitting under trees is another of the regular practices I enjoy. It is inspiring to see beautiful Redwoods, also known as the "wisdom keepers" of California.

There are many benefits derived from sitting under trees. Sitting under trees isn't just a new age or "hippy" thing. It has been practiced for thousands of years. Buddha became enlightened while sitting under a tree.

Many yogis and rishis sit under trees to receive profound wisdom that they then share with the world.

When I sit under a tree I almost feel like I am back in my mother's lap, feeling unconditionally loved.

Trees provide us with so much more than oxygen, food, shade, shelter, cubby-houses, places to play and be creative; they also provide a place for us to sit and relax, and appreciate the beauty of our surroundings.

The next time you have five minutes free to recharge your tired body and mind, try sitting comfortably under a beautiful tree and acknowledge what you can see, hear, touch, and smell.

Gently bring your attention to your breath; take slower, deeper breaths in, and slower, controlled breaths out. Continue to focus on your breath, and allow any wandering thoughts to drift by, as if they're on a floating cloud, without engaging with them.

As you continue to sit, your mind will want to wander. When you catch your mind wandering to other thoughts of what's been or what hasn't happened yet, gently bring your mind back to you sitting under the tree and what you can see now.

Then gently bring your focus back to your breath, take slower, deeper breaths in, and slower, controlled breaths out.

Relax.

You may close your eyes if you want, and smile, softly relaxing your jaw and face. Feel your shoulders and body relax, and breathe deeply.

The more you practice mindfulness, the better you will become at taking a break from your mind, being free from worry, accepting what is without judgment, connecting to your own inner peace, and the richer your life will be.

Message From an Old Tree

I was once sitting under a tree when I felt a profound moment of deep connection.

Here is the message that came from the tree:

There was a tree more than 2500 years old. This tree saw many civilizations; civilizations that planted trees and those that cut down trees.

Civilizations that loved animals, and those that killed animals.

When this old tree was falling down, there were new, small trees, rising to support it.

As this tree fell down it was telling me that its love for humanity was in the past, in the present, and will be forever in the future.

Love, from tree.

Blessing to the Four Directions

The Blessing to the Four Directions has its roots in Native American and many other cultures.

It is the belief that human beings are tied to all things in nature. It is this belief which assigned virtues to the four cardinal directions; East, South, West, and North.

In many ancient religious traditions, it is customary to bring a service of worship or celebration by calling on the four directions.

This is a way of symbolically inviting all of creation to be present and take part in the festivities.

Each of these blessings from the four cardinal directions emphasizes those things that help one build a happy and successful union. Yet they are only tools—tools which one must use together in order to create what you seek in this union.

Oh Great Spirit of the North, we come to you and ask for the strength and power to bear what is cold and harsh in life.

We come like the buffalo, ready to receive the winds that truly can be overwhelming at times.

Whatever is cold and uncertain in life, we ask you to give us the strength to bear it. Do not let the winter blow us away.

Oh Spirit of Life and Spirit of the North, we ask you for strength and warmth.

Oh Great Spirit of the East, we turn to you where the sun comes up, from where the power of light and refreshment come.

Everything that is born comes up in this direction; the birth of babies, the birth of puppies, the birth of ideas, and the birth of friendship.

Let there be the light.

Oh Spirit of the East, let the color of fresh rising in our life be glory to you.

Oh Great Spirit of the South, spirit of all that is warm and gentle and refreshing, we ask you to give us this spirit of growth, of fertility, of gentleness.

Caress us with a cool breeze when the days are hot.

Give us seeds that the flowers, trees, and fruits of the earth may grow.

Give us the warmth of good friendships.

Oh Spirit of the South, send the warmth and the growth of your blessings.

Oh Great Spirit of the West, where the sun goes down each day to come up the next, we turn to you in praise of sunsets and in thanksgiving for changes.

You are the great colored sunset of the red west, which illuminates us.

You are the powerful cycle, which pulls us to transformation.

We ask for the blessings of the sunset.

Keep us open to life's changes.

This prayer for the four directions was inspired by Native American cultures.

To all the wisdom keepers of the world, and to all sentient beings I dedicate this prayer.

Acknowledgements

Firstly, I would like to express gratitude to my parents for
their love and kindness.

To my siblings Santosh, Krishna and Sunita,
I am grateful for your unfailing support.

From the bottom of my heart, I am most grateful to Cindy Ma
who's has supported me in all things. It was because of her
that I traveled to United states, opened a Thanka gallery,
produced a flute album and wrote this very book.

Special thanks to my dear brother Sam Wise who despite his
being in retreat, has helped me review this work.

Also to my Bay area community and those who have
supported the gallery all these years.

With deepest respect, I would like to acknowledge Jog
Bahadur Gauchan. He has guided me unfailingly on my
entrepreneurial journey.

Thank you Advanced Publishing for publishing this book.

I am forever grateful for the Dharma teachings and spiritual
presence of my root guru Penor Rinpoche, as well as and all
the masters of Nyignma and other traditions
such as Trulshik Rinpoche, Chatral Sangye
Dorje Rinpoche, Gyalwang Drukpa
and Mindrolling Jetsün Khandro Rinpoche.

SBOOKS

Standard Books:
An imprint of Advanced Publishing LLC
Alamo, California

CPSIA information can be obtained
at www.ICGtesting.com
Printed in the USA
FSHW010003131219
64808FS